WHAT DO *men* WANT?

REAL MEN EXPOSE THEIR
Needs & Desires

Hallie Potocki

CASABLANCA PRESS®
A DIVISION OF SOURCEBOOKS, INC.®
NAPERVILLE, ILLINOIS

Published by Sourcebooks, Inc.
P.O. Box 4410, Naperville, Illinois 60567-4410
(630) 961-3900
FAX: (630) 961-2168

Library of Congress Cataloging-in-Publication Data

Potocki, Hallie.
    What do men want?: real men expose their needs and desires / Hallie Potocki.
      p. cm.
    ISBN 1-57071-591-2 (alk. paper)
    1. Men. 2. Man-woman relationships. I. Title

    HQ1090.P67 2000
    305.31—dc21

                                       00-044045

Printed and bound in the United States of America
DR 10 9 8 7 6 5 4 3 2 1

TABLE OF CONTENTS

INTRODUCTION

First off, nothing fancy. I stepped out of my usually demure and wholly sensible self for what just couldn't be described as more than a moment—honest—and put together this kind of no-holds-barred, men-only, twenty-question survey focusing on sex and man-woman relationships. The crazy part, and the reason for the book, is that about 250 guys actually went and filled the things out!

The long version of how I got into this would probably best be hashed over feet-up with a couple of beers, but the mercifully shorter one is that I'm recently divorced and "starting over," and although always aware, technically, at any rate, that they were supposed to be people and all, found myself craving a more substantial handle on who and what they—men, I mean—were really all about. And, succumbing to the very brief lapse mentioned earlier, decided I would just simply gulp hard and ask the creatures themselves.

I handed out questionnaires to everyone from smokers on breaks in front of office buildings to poor misbegotten souls happening to stop next to me at a traffic light, to, primarily through the blissful ease and anonymity of cyberspace, some of the more candid, charming, and reflective members of America Online.

I thought I'd get back a lot of junk to sift through—a lot of pranks, bravado, and "Sure, baby, I'll answer your questions with this," kind of stuff—but I didn't. There was none of that. The responses I received were instead forthright, intelligent, articulate, and engaging. A close read will reveal voices honest and textured and not so readily found. Respondents' ages ranged from twenty-two to seventy-two years—average is thirty-eight—and participants came from forty-seven states. Their occupations go across the board.

Other than occasionally fleshing out an especially engaging or provocative comment with a brief follow-up dialogue with its writer, my intention is to let each participant speak with as little intrusion as possible. If a book can simply be a nice place to hang out, that is what I would like this one to be.

I have learned that breasts don't have to be big, or at least not that big; teeth can really hurt when doing, well, you know (and they love doing it to women, too); semipublic sex and mild bondage are right up there in fantasy with the ubiquitous threesome; they aren't only about sex, or at least not totally; are capable of caring; enjoy getting a phone call in spite of *The Rules*; and when you cut them, they kind of, somewhat, sort of, almost, bleed. Also, real is better than fake and the importance of laughter and a smile cannot be overestimated.

The honesty and intimacy shared in the answers to my questionnaire have allowed for quite an experience. A part of me has probably fallen in love with each and every one of these guys.

Part One

SHARING

THE

REMOTE

Men AND
Women REALLY
PART WAYS WHEN
IT COMES TO...

Sharing feelings or talking about them. Men generally
run like hell.
—*Architect, 33*

Pretty much anything, but, specifically, the significance
of a good night of sex. Guys: a good night of sex.
Girls: the bond that unites two individuals for life.
—*Disc jockey, 29*

Men

AND

Women

REALLY

PART

WAYS

WHEN

IT COMES

TO...

Understanding the other's motivation and meaning in a conversation. I say, "No," she hears, "Maybe." I say, "Sure" and she asks, "Why?" or, "You don't really want to, do you?"

—*Plumber, 35*

Sex, food, cars, children, houses, clothes, TV, radio, restaurants, movies, pets, society.

—*Psychologist, 40*

Money, emotions, practicality, logic.

🖎 *Follow-up: Money's mentioned a lot...how so?*

It's the spending of it...I think this all relates to the inference that men are more practical than women. Most men go shopping when they need something and they go specifically for that item. Every woman I can think of loves to go shopping. If they see something nice, they will buy it. They even love to "window shop" when they don't have money! If you can't afford to buy something, why eat your heart out?!

—*Accountant, 43*

Asking directions. Seriously, I don't think there is any generalization that could be made in response to this question. Men and women come in all varieties, I've found.

—*Financial consultant, 48*

How uncomplicated men are…

—*College instructor, 42*

To most men, the big picture is all that matters, with women, it seems to be the little things. A woman can never see the big picture if she cannot get past the anger and resentment of not "getting" the little things. Men screw up by saying, "Why are you getting upset? It is nothing."

—*Environmental activist, 37*

Communication. Women talk in code. Men don't talk at all.

—*Media consultant, 42*

Men
AND
Women
REALLY
PART
WAYS
WHEN
IT COMES
TO…

5

Men

AND

Women

REALLY

PART

WAYS

WHEN

IT COMES

TO...

Probably the biggest difference is in how they judge people. Women, despite their reputation as nurturers, are much more critical of men than vice versa. I work in an office with almost all women, and to hear them tell it, all men are idiots, pigs, oafs, and cheats. When men sit around discussing women, we always end up at the same place—"What do they want?"
—*Events producer, 34*

How to resolve conflicts.
—*Corporate manager, 47*

Men can really be turned on by beautiful women they've never seen before and desire to have sex with them. Most women don't seem to get turned on in this way with strangers.
—*Contractor, 42*

What they talk about.
—*Account representative, 34*

Men and women really part ways when it comes to the goals of communication. Women do not communicate to identify or solve problems. They communicate to sound out their feelings or to make feelings known. Men communicate to solve problems. Often when a woman has a problem, a man will become frustrated because when he asks what he can do about it, a woman will respond, "Nothing." A woman may become frustrated by a man who is constantly trying to "fix" her.

—*Computer support technician, 28*

Ideas of intimacy and commitment.

—*Supervisor, 37*

The way a partner is treated. When I am tender, loving, and romantic to my woman, she behaves as though I were inferior. When she is that way to me, I feel tearfully and poetically grateful to her and to God for giving her to me. Now I know enough to cater to the bit of masochist in my next woman.

—*Engineer, 48*

Men AND *Women* REALLY PART WAYS WHEN IT COMES TO...

7

Men
AND
Women
REALLY

PART

WAYS

WHEN

IT COMES

TO...

Priorities! Most women do not understand the importance of work. Not just from an income perspective, but that it keeps your mind sharp, keeps you up on current events, and helps to drive that passion for life we are all striving to embrace. I meet so many women who think they can quit work, take the summer off, go part time—just because they are married. And the little things that get their panties in a bunch is just incredible! From what they are wearing, to socializing, to sports—you name it.
—*Financial planner, 35*

The ability to manipulate the other. Women study men much more carefully than men study women.
—*Writer, 37*

What they expect when entering a relationship. Men accept what the woman is now, knowing that this may deteriorate...women see a man as a "diamond in the rough" that she may be able to mold into her ideal mate.
—*Geologist, 44*

Talking for no specific reason.

—*Musician, 46*

Sex: men want it almost all the time and women want romance and to be entertained most of the time.

—*Certified public accountant, 33*

How involved men get with sports. I have met very few women who truly understand how I can get so totally involved in a sporting event that it can change me from a nice guy to a raging lunatic.

—*Information director, 32*

Coarseness, drinking, and fighting.

—*Electronic engineer, 51*

Views of life. Despite gains in equality, men still measure their lives by what they do and women primarily by their family life (whether single, married, with or without children).

—*Real estate broker, 45*

Men AND *Women* REALLY PART WAYS WHEN IT COMES TO...

Men

AND

Women

REALLY

PART

WAYS

WHEN

IT COMES

TO...

For what they enjoy (e.g., shopping as a leisure activity), what they remember (emotions vs. things), and what they notice.

—Attorney, 45

Intuition.

—Firefighter, 43

IS IT TRUE THAT A *Woman* SHOULD NEVER INITIATE A PHONE CALL TO A *Man*?

What utter crap—what century is this we're living in again?

—Self-employed, 43

Just plain dumb. It reminds me of one of my favorite quotes:"As long as women get their information about men from other women, they will always get it wrong."

—Outdoor/rafting guide, 38

Total BS. We love the thrill of the chase, but it is often incredibly stimulating to be chased by a desirable woman...I personally love an aggressive woman.

—Carpenter, 30

IS IT
TRUE
THAT A
Woman
SHOULD
NEVER
INITIATE A
PHONE
CALL TO
A *Man*?

Communication is too important to waste on protocol.
—*Accountant, 35*

Maybe other guys. I like a woman to speak her mind. If she wants to call, then call. Where did you get this thrill of the chase stereotype…from a James Bond movie?
—*Construction foreman, 38*

I totally disagree. Looking back over my life, some of my best, most successful relationships have been with women who made the first move.
—*Website designer, 44*

I don't like the "chase" thing. Wouldn't even know how anymore…I was married too long. I think I would just prefer honesty…not games.
—*Warehouse manager, 41*

BS! Guys are as shy and cowardly as anyone. If a woman likes a man and gets a good vibe, don't wait. I hate the head games. Some Emily Post–type creature thought that up a long time ago when the game was different. Lose the handbook—take a chance!
—*Financial planner, 35*

I hate to be the one who has to do the chasing all the time! I wouldn't mind being chased once in a while. It is not about the chase, anyway…it is about the amazing things that happen when you connect!
—*Teacher, 35*

Complete BS. Guys do love "the thrill of the chase" and, heck, I've even justified going very slowly with some women because the wooing was more exciting that the winning; however, if I was interested in a woman and she called me, I wouldn't say, "Oh no, too easy." That's for chumps and morons. It's not like she showed up at my door with her slippers and moved in. The game isn't completely over, just getting easier.
—*Advertising project manager, 26*

IS IT TRUE THAT A *Woman* SHOULD NEVER INITIATE A PHONE CALL TO A *Man*?

Is it true that a *Woman* should never initiate a phone call to a *Man*?

Women calling me…Yes, I'm open to this and don't think any less of her for pursuing me.
—*Financial consultant, 51*

I love it when a woman calls me. It makes me feel special. Makes me feel that she is thinking about me. I do love the chase, but at my age, I like a little response.
—*Industrial supplier, 40*

There's nothing more flattering to a man than the attentions of a pretty, intelligent woman. I have been thrilled by a simple touch on my arm during a conversation, let alone a phone call.
—*Retired advertising executive, 61*

Balance. Chase sometimes and be chased sometimes. Use tact!
—*Computer technician, 44*

A guy who likes chasing that much should never be allowed to catch.

—*Software designer, 34*

Hell, no. I like my women to call me, especially if it is long distance.

—*Business owner, 45*

Guys like being called just as much as women.

—*Production worker, 39*

Men like to be called, but not smothered, and a woman should not overdo it.

—*Administrator, 53*

Wrong…I like to be pursued, hate to be stalked.

—*Stockbroker, 28*

Let him work in peace. Call him in the evenings after he has wound down.

—*Corporate manager, 42*

IS IT TRUE THAT A *Woman* SHOULD NEVER INITIATE A PHONE CALL TO A *Man*?

IS IT

TRUE

THAT A

Woman

SHOULD

NEVER

INITIATE A

PHONE

CALL TO

A *Man*?

To think that one person should not make a move to another is to deny the possibility of finding the person for you. A lot of great friendships and relationships never happened because of that type of thinking.

—*Journalist, 49*

I don't mind initiating, but on the other hand, when a woman makes herself available there's no question she's interested, alleviating the prerequisite hoop dance that generally goes along with dating (something I truly detest).

—*Contractor, 38*

I don't mind the calls, it tells me that the woman is actually interested and that I can continue the pursuit. However, I do like to be the chaser once I know there is true interest! At that point, I would agree with the statement.

—*Emergency medical technician, 29*

The man might not know she's interested. Besides, why should we always be the one to risk rejection. Hard-to-get is a stupid, outdated mind game based on a "good girls don't do it" mentality.

—*Software engineer, 31*

Ridiculous. Many men fear, greatly, rejection from a woman in whom they have an interest…so much so, in many cases, that they'd rather never know whether the woman is interested than learn that she isn't.

—*Writer, 48*

The woman can be aggressive, but "neediness" is not taken well…a woman can turn the chase around any time!

—*Electrical engineer, 49*

Yes, there's an element of sport involved, but speaking from a guy's standpoint, it's absolutely fine if the woman takes the initiative at times. No, we don't see it as a sign of victory or anything like that, just a sign of caring or mutual attraction.

—*Military serviceman, 27*

IS IT TRUE THAT A *Woman* SHOULD NEVER INITIATE A PHONE CALL TO A *Man*?

IS IT

TRUE

THAT A

Woman

SHOULD

NEVER

INITIATE A

PHONE

CALL TO

A *Man*?

I think that it's great when a woman lets me know that she's interested and willing to date me. A friendly call to chat is fine, even asking for the first date. But don't hound me for my every available bit of time off to be together. If I'm interested, I will definitely find a way to be with you.

—*Slot machine technician, 43*

Hell, no. I'm too old for games. If you want me, let me know. Please!!

—*Geologist, 44*

Wrong! I think it's good for a woman to call a man, but not all the time. It's also up to the man to call the woman, too. I'd say it's a 50/50 thing…but don't overdo it with the phone calls.

—*Electronic engineer, 52*

Almost always a delightful experience.

—*Self-employed, 44*

IS A TRULY PLATONIC FRIENDSHIP WITH A *Woman* POSSIBLE?

Yes, right after sex (just kidding). I have a lot of female friends.

—*Sound technician, 34*

It is absolutely possible. All relationships between men and women should start that way. Friends first.

—*Computer technical support rep, 35*

IS A

TRULY

PLATONIC

FRIENDSHIP

WITH A

Woman

POSSIBLE?

Definitely. I get along better with women than men. Women's hearts and souls are softer and gentler, as is mine. Maybe I should have been a woman… maybe in another life.
—*Stockbroker, 28*

I've had several platonic relationships, but like Billy Crystal said in *When Harry Met Sally*, you pretty much want to sleep with them, anyway.
—*Mechanic, 36*

Yes. I have had one for seven years. She is my best friend.
—*Business owner, 49*

Yes, in theory. No, in experience.
—*Regional account manager, 53*

I believe it's possible, but difficult. There is a fine line between a deep, meaningful friendship with a woman and the feelings of intimacy that seem to develop from that friendship. I think there comes a time when there is a natural desire to share more and explore the depth of the friendship in less than platonic ways. Tough question.

—Aircraft maintenance technician, 31

Yes, it is most definitely possible to have a woman as your friend for life.

—Firefighter, 41

I have a couple of female friends who are just that, nothing more…no particular reason, just that we have established mutual trust and really good friendships.

—Electrician, 32

No. Too bad. But no. Sexual speculation is always in the background, on both parts. Whether conscious or not.

—Financial consultant, 48

Yes…but only if there is no real physical attraction. Otherwise, no way!!!

—Retail manager, 31

Scintillating statistics:

Out of 227 men, 153 thought a platonic relationship was possible, 44 thought maybe, and 30 thought no.

IS A TRULY PLATONIC FRIENDSHIP WITH A *Woman* POSSIBLE?

IS A

TRULY

PLATONIC

FRIENDSHIP

WITH A

Woman

POSSIBLE?

Absolutely. With my mother.

—*Photographer, 45*

I believe it is, but as a divorced guy, I think many women have underlying intentions. Ego? Possibly.

—*Carpenter, 30*

I think sex-buddies are becoming more and more popular. No jealousy between partners, purely friendship, but they still have sex together.

—*Salesman, 28*

I had a platonic relationship for years with a wonderful lady, until one day....We are still great friends, but, no, I do not think a truly platonic relationship can exist.

—*Business owner, 39*

I've had some very close relationships with women I never bedded. I also still have some with women with whom I have been intimate and that have evolved into the platonic category.

—*Musician, 45*

Certainly. A platonic relationship is possible if (1) she is over 80, or (2) she is ugly and dumb, but loves to pick up the tab in a sports bar.
—*Material damages analyst, 43*

No!
—*Business owner, 36*

Absolutely yes, after the man exhausts the possibilities for a sexual relationship!
—*Engineer, 39*

I'm not sure. Probably not in my case.
—*Salesman, 41*

Absolutely. Included is usually a lot of harmless flirtation.
—*UAW die maker, 45*

Yes, but may have to be reminded it's only platonic from time to time.
—*Real estate appraiser, 46*

IS A TRULY PLATONIC FRIENDSHIP WITH A *Woman* POSSIBLE?

IS A

TRULY

PLATONIC

FRIENDSHIP

WITH A

Woman

POSSIBLE?

I have several female friends I have known since grade school with whom I remain friends to this day. I have more female friends than male friends.
—*Information director, 32*

My second wife and I have a truly platonic friendship six years after our divorce.
—*Retired, 62*

Sure. I have many women friends at work and they are all platonic. Why do friends have to be the same gender?
—*Optician, 52*

Only if both parties understand the relationship as such. Usually, one or both have their feelings change.
—*Supervisor, 36*

Very possible and very fulfilling. When you have any questions about a woman, who better to ask. I believe it takes a mature male to truly be friends with a woman. It takes more time to get to know a woman. Two guys can seem to hit it off just by liking the same sports team or type of car. With women, it takes more. You have to factor in emotion and feelings.

—*Landscaper, 31*

Very possible, but these days most men are out for sex, not a friend. I have several female friends with whom I have never slept, but I have been told I am not your average male by many of them.

—*Mechanic, 26*

IS A

TRULY

PLATONIC

FRIENDSHIP

WITH A

Woman

POSSIBLE?

Part Two

JUST

LOOKING,

THANKS

THE MOST ALLURING PART OF A *Woman's* BODY HAS GOT TO BE...

Legs—don't know why—been that way since the first grade.
—*Art director, 38*

Eyes. I also like legs, breasts, lips (both pair), and neck and shoulders—hmmmm, waist, butt, toes...damn, that question has me cookin'.
—*Contractor, 44*

THE MOST

ALLURING

PART OF A

Woman's

BODY

HAS GOT

TO BE...

Her butt...I love a tight, firm rear end...makes my knees weak and my mouth water. That's how I met my ex in high school. She was coming out of a car, butt first, and I told a buddy, "Do you see that? I will have it before the year is over." I did not count on falling in love with who the fine ass was attached to. We were married before the year was over and were for almost 17 years.
—*Plumber, 35*

It's the area of a woman's stomach between her navel down to the beginning of her pubic hair...it's not even bad if she has a tiny bit of pooch there.
—*Attorney, 53*

Hair, eyes, breasts, hips, butt, legs, ankles, and feet. In that order.
—*Network engineer, 38*

The quiche eaters' answer would be her mind, and I do enjoy that, but, physically, rear end and legs.

🍂 *Follow-up: Over and over I'm hearing that legs and butts are as popular an attraction as breasts, and that breast size isn't necessarily all that important...so why the media emphasis on breasts and all the interest in implants?*

My guess is that it's a self-esteem issue. Women want to be attractive to men, so they try the obvious thing to get attention. Even though I'm not a "breast" man, they are one of the first things I'll notice about a woman. A woman with larger breasts is going to get noticed. It's sort of a Darwin thing I guess. Sort of survival of the fittest...or in this case, biggest.

—*Teacher, 35*

Her eyes, face, breasts, butt, legs… I am a guy, and I don't need Viagra… all this stuff works for me.

—*Financial consultant, 50*

Scintillating statistics:

men mentioned:
eyes 56 times
breasts 35 times
legs 35 times
butt 35 times
face 24 times
total package 17 times
smile 15 times
mouth/lips 15 times
mind 11 times
neck 11 times
hair 7 times
feet 6 times

THE MOST ALLURING PART OF A *Woman's* BODY HAS GOT TO BE…

THE MOST

ALLURING

PART OF A

Woman's

BODY

HAS GOT

TO BE...

Butt, lips, eyes, smell, I love women.
—*Student, 24*

Her eyes. Legs can entice, a great butt can attract, a nice pair of breasts can distract, a good body can drive a man wild, but to truly attract me, a woman needs a spark—intelligence, wit, zest, charm, some kind of extra umph, not entirely physical. And the only place to see that is in the eyes.
—*Computer technical support rep, 28*

Here is where you'll think I'm nuts. For me, it's the ears. They're always hidden behind the hair so that when uncovered, it's like exposing something forbidden.
—*Database maintenance rep, 37*

Toss up, eyes and hair, or long legs (34" +).
—*Architect, 33*

Her back. Don't have a reason…just like backs.
—*Electrician, 32*

I like it all, but she doesn't have to be a Playmate.

—*Firefighter, 26*

The skin of her legs, above the knee.

—*Bioinformation specialist, 43*

I really like all parts of a woman's body, but unlike many acquaintances of mine, I have no "type." I know guys who like big boobs, long legs, trim tushies, tiny ladies, tubby ladies, or long, flowing hair (singly or in various combinations). Me? I like whatever equipment comes standard on the lady I'm currently in love with.

—*Retired advertising executive, 61*

Anything that is uncovered at the time.

—*Engineer, 66*

The face is where it starts, then I go to the mind.

—*Administrator, 53*

THE MOST ALLURING PART OF A *Woman's* BODY HAS GOT TO BE...

33

THE MOST

ALLURING

PART OF A

Woman's

BODY

HAS GOT

TO BE...

Her eyes and smile, and of course, her skin—the feel of it, the smell of it, the taste of it—whether it is her neck, her shoulders, her stomach... shall I go on?
—*Operations manager, 38*

It all depends on the woman...and that is not intended to evade the question. I think it really does depend on the woman, and is different for every one of them.
—*Certified public accountant, 33*

Ah, here is where I show how I've grown over the years. In the past, I was definitely a breast kind of guy. I still am, but now the smile is what first will turn me on and make me want to get to know someone a little better.
—*Teacher, 50*

Small waist, flat stomach, and looks good in semi-tight jeans.
—*Martial arts instructor, 44*

I am very turned on by that one tendon on the upper inner thigh…very warm, moist, and kissable. A great place to visit.

—*Website developer, 42*

Her breasts and the mystery surrounding them. The softness, contour, shape, feel, and smell. I don't care about the size. Nothing is more erotic than to have one's head hugged to a woman's chest and the aromas and mystery just overwhelm you.

✎ *Follow-up: A lot of you guys are saying breast size is not necessarily that important, so, apologies to Howard Stern, I've been asking how come we're always hearing so much about big "cans"?*

I think the importance of a woman's breast size is an issue because of the few people who control media. We are inundated by images of large breasted women and hunks in ads, pictorials, etc. They portray successful people as having these attributes. In a lot of homes, the woman was told that she wasn't good enough or that she needed a man to complete her. How then could she not think that the images pro-

THE MOST ALLURING PART OF A *Woman's* BODY HAS GOT TO BE...

THE MOST

ALLURING

PART OF A

Woman's

BODY

HAS GOT

TO BE...

jected would somehow make her more complete and accepted?

—*Electronic engineer, 48*

When talking a specific part, her neck line. It's one of the softest, smoothest areas on a woman's body and knowing that it is a very effective erogenous zone excites me even more.

—*Musician, 28*

The most alluring part of a woman's body is her ability to use it.

—*Police officer, 36*

Long, slender legs.

—*Retired, 72*

Boobs—the bigger, the better.

—*Stockbroker, 28*

Lower back.

—*Human resources manager, 33*

Soft skin on her hips.

—*UAW die maker, 44*

Calves.

—*Engineer, 41*

Lips.

—*Estate planner, 52*

Belly button.

🔖 *Follow-up: Belly button?*

It makes an enticing target area for kissing, nibbling, licking, etc. Plus, I'm a cuddler, so I like to kiss my way down to a woman's navel and rest my head on her stomach.

—*Military serviceman, 22*

Shape and skin.

—*Retired, 62*

Brain.

—*Teacher, 50*

THE MOST ALLURING PART OF A *Woman's* BODY HAS GOT TO BE...

MY THOUGHTS ON *breast implants* ARE...

They are for the woman, not for me. Having no "type," I have been in love with women who were flat-chested, women with perfect natural breasts, and one woman with implants. I was, in turn, crazy about them all.

—*Retired advertising executive, 61*

Why??? The smallest real things are better than the best looking fakes.

—*Military serviceman, 22*

My

THOUGHTS

ON *breast*

implants

ARE...

It's a personal decision a woman makes for her own reasons. It's not something she should ever do for someone else, especially the man in her life. Breast implants are a self-esteem issue and if a woman will feel better about herself if she has larger breasts (whether or not breast size should make a difference as to how a woman feels about herself is irrelevant...it does for a lot of women), she should consider doing it.

—*Operations manager, 38*

Personally, I can't understand why a woman would want them, no matter what her breast size. But if it helps her in any way, then sure...after all, we can do whatever we please with our bodies. My attraction to a woman would have nothing to do with her breast size.

—*Military serviceman, 27*

Nope; no; nada; don't do it; yuck; gag me; gross; pass on it; bad idea. I like large-breasted women very much, but a natural B is far better than a fake D.

—*Accountant, 38*

Not necessary, but the one relationship I have had with a woman with breast implants was great and they were absolutely beautiful.

—*Retired commercial pilot, 53*

Too dangerous—I'm happy with a good set of nipples!

—*Retired, 68*

Fun to look at in the movies or at a strip club, but not something I'd want a partner/girlfriend of mine to have. Of course, if she's gorgeous, interested in me, and just happens to have had them, that doesn't mean I'm gonna send her on her way. It's a preference, not a rule.

—*Advertising project manager, 26*

Full breasts are delightful, but I would rather have a woman who has nothing but perky nipples than those hard, phony things—big thumbs down. I am a butt man, anyway. Do they do have implants for that part of the body? Women should focus on that area more—gotta feel real, though!

—*Software engineer, 41*

MY THOUGHTS ON *breast implants* ARE...

41

MY

THOUGHTS

ON *breast*

implants

ARE...

They make me uncomfortable. I think they are scary and a big health risk. I don't want to be with some-one who is so uncomfortable with herself that she would have to do that.
—*Teacher, 35*

Why bother? The nipples are the best part.
—*Martial arts instructor, 44*

Got to be one of the sickest inventions ever.
—*Career coach, 53*

I cannot understand why a person would inject a foreign substance in her body for an image that is totally sexist and demeaning to women. Have we as men beat women's self image so badly that they would cause harm to themselves for an acceptable profile that only a jerk could think was great?
—*Electronic engineer, 48*

Take 'em or leave 'em. I prefer natural, but...
—*Accountant, 33*

Oh, if only women knew how stupid they look with those. Of course, we look pretty stupid staring at them. But lots of us like Medium a lot better than XXL.
—*Media consultant, 41*

It's the lady's choice. I'm a brain, legs, and butt man.
—*Health care provider, 41*

If they make her feel better about herself and she wants them, then it is fine with me.
—*Dentist, 45*

Hate the fake way they feel.
—*Account representative, 36*

Who cares? More than a mouthful is a waste and the nipples are always real. I have heard that sensitivity is lost for the woman with implants. Why would you want to give up sensitivity for size?
—*Landscaper, 31*

Scintillating statistics:

**Do men like breast implants? (out of 250 responses)
no/not necessary, 139
okay/neutral, 76
like 'em, 27
no response, 8**

MY THOUGHTS ON *breast implants* ARE...

MY

THOUGHTS

ON *breast*

implants

ARE...

They are fine—I dated a gal who had them and her tits were firm and ripe, and her nipples were in a state of constant arousal—and she was 52!

—*Business owner, 58*

Nope, don't like them. Do the best with what you have and shine in other areas. Enhance all the positives to overwhelm the negatives. Anyway, if the nipples are sensitive, a man can be happy.

—*Computer technical support rep, 29*

A waste of money coupled with unnecessary health risks…love yourself, would 'ya?

—*Carpenter, 30*

My lady had reconstructive surgery after a double mastectomy. She looks fantastic. Good cleavage is a plus. Men like to see it. So go for it!

—*UAW die maker, 45*

I think it's a woman's body and she is free to do with it what she pleases. I know several women who were very self-conscious over their lack of breasts— after their implants their self-confidence increased many times over.

—*Salesman, 32*

If a woman feels she wants them because she really is insecure about her breasts, then she should do it. But I don't care for the really large breasts that some women get. In those cases, they just look sleazy to me. And, of course, if someone did it for medical purposes, i.e., lost a breast due to surgery, etc., then I would truly accept it. To me, breast size is unimportant.

—*Training manager, 41*

MY

THOUGHTS

ON *breast*

implants

ARE...

45

THE THING THAT TURNS ME ON MOST/ TURNS ME OFF MOST ABOUT A *Woman* IS...

The one thing that turns me on most about a woman is her smile. A beautiful smile can warm an entire room. Conversely, nothing turns me off more than when a woman speaks like the proverbial truck driver (and hearing some of their mouths, I'd have to apologize to the truck drivers).

—*Basketball coach, 39*

THE

THING THAT

TURNS ME

ON MOST/

TURNS ME

OFF MOST

ABOUT A

Woman

IS...

I assume this is after knowing each other for some time, and after the male "visual" thing has calmed down a bit. Then it is closed-mindedness for turn off and intelligence for turn on. Or did you want surface things like "eye makeup"?
—*Businessman, 46*

Physically: turn on is usually an expressive face with soulful eyes. Turn off: um…facial hair. Intellectually: turn on is someone with a great sly wit. Turn off: someone who never thinks beyond the first superficial layer.
—*Film editor, 26*

Turns me on: attractive, classy, sexy, independent lady. Turns me off: lack of mutual respect.
—*Engineer, 42*

If you get one thousand responses, you'll probably get one thousand answers to this one. What turns me on about a woman is depth, complexity, contradiction, and spirituality, but not in a religious sense. I like strong, self-confident women who also know how to let their guard down and take the risk with me to be vulnerable (because we all are vulnerable at times, no matter how strong an exterior we display). I like playfulness and women who don't take themselves too seriously. What turns me off…well, I guess the opposites of the things that turn me on, though that sounds like a bit of a cop out.

—*Marketer, 38*

Turn on: outgoing, likes to laugh, and nice butt! Turn off: loud, obnoxious, and selfish.

—*Attorney, 39*

On: simplicity and sensitivity or fabulous wealth and big breasts. Off: vanity and materialism or STDs and jealous husbands.

—*Software engineer, 40*

Turn on: kindness to anything—people, pets, me. Turn off: insincerity, coldness.

—*Landscaper, 31*

THE THING THAT TURNS ME ON MOST/ TURNS ME OFF MOST ABOUT A *Woman* IS…

49

THE

THING THAT

TURNS ME

ON MOST/

TURNS ME

OFF MOST

ABOUT A

Woman

IS...

Turn on: first, hate to say it, is looks—her smile, her eyes, her hair, her feet, and her hands! Past that, it's what she does, what her passion is, what risks she's taken, how active she is, what gets her excited! Turn off: prejudices, lack of passion, unwillingness to care for herself—like not exercising or eating right!
—*Financial planner, 35*

Turn on: total exhibitionistic abandonment. Turn off: attempts to make me feel responsible for healing her emotional wounds.
—*Retired advertising executive, 61*

Turn on: a woman who can look me straight in my eyes while we talk. Turn off: when we are in a crowd or at a party, she forgets to include me, even when I'm sitting right next to her.
—*Retired, 67*

On: a woman who loves sex! Off: smoking!
—*Supervisor, 47*

Turn offs: money grubbing is first. Loud and crass is in second place. Fat means she is someone else's lover. Turn ons: svelte, very intelligent, highly sensual/sexual, middle-class social values (same as mine), an active interest in me as a person, mind, and body (all three).

🖎 *Follow-up: Hmmm…"very intelligent." What ever happened to, "Men never make passes at girls who wear glasses?"*

A woman who is a complete drain on a man's resources is not attractive except maybe to the guy who is really unsure of himself. A good relationship—in a man's eyes, and I believe in most women's eyes—is a partnership where both gain more than they put in. When either one feels they are putting in more than they are gaining, he or she will either leave or get very angry. Utterly helpless females give a guy the feeling of being used.

—*Salesman, 49*

THE
THING THAT
TURNS ME
ON MOST/
TURNS ME
OFF MOST
ABOUT A
Woman
IS…

THE

THING THAT

TURNS ME

ON MOST/

TURNS ME

OFF MOST

ABOUT A

Woman

IS...

Turn on: when she looks sexy in a t-shirt after just waking up. Turn off: too much makeup, frills, and big hair.

—*Electrician, 32*

Turn on: flirtatious, touchy-feely. Turn off: cold, not affectionate.

—*Systems engineer, 45*

On? If she lets me know that she's turned on. Turns me off? Hmmmm…when she's inhibited and shows it. I'm not into shy women. I prefer the type of gal who can intimidate men with her looks and brains.

—*Self-employed, 38*

Turn on: being honest and direct. Turn off: pretending to be someone other than who she is.

—*Promoter, 32*

Turn on: she goes out of her way to look sexy for me. Turn off: when after a while in a relationship she doesn't care about looking good anymore.

—*Business owner, 49*

Turn on: someone who wants me for exactly who and what I am. Turn off: someone who needs to get something out of me which I may or may not be able to give.

—*Writer, 37*

Depends on what kind of answer you want. Body part? Personality trait? To be sure, I'll give you both. 1) Smile. I would have said legs, but I thought about it, and while I love nice legs, I have seen leggy women who didn't smile and was turned off, and I've seen women with ordinary legs who did, and was turned on. There is a lot that goes into my considering a woman attractive, but the smile is the canvas on which all other details are seen. 2) Quick wit. If a woman can't kibitz (shoot the bull, keep up a lively conversation), then the interaction becomes tired in a hurry.

—*Advertising project manager, 26*

THE

THING THAT

TURNS ME

ON MOST/

TURNS ME

OFF MOST

ABOUT A

Woman

IS...

THE

THING THAT

TURNS ME

ON MOST/

TURNS ME

OFF MOST

ABOUT A

Woman

IS...

Turn on: genuine interest. Turn off: being phony or wrapped up in herself and, most of all, immaturity and distrust.

—*Healthcare aide, 27*

Turn on: femininity, beauty, subtly sexy. Turn off: clingy, desperate, jealous.

☙ *Follow-up: What about the allure of the "helpless" female?*

I don't really believe in the helpless female. I think that many women pretend to be helpless to boost the insecure male ego. I personally would rather the woman be herself. There are women smarter, stronger, and more in touch with reality than I may be. It doesn't scare me. It impresses me. I don't look for someone who is codependent...the more confident each is, the better and stronger the relationship will be.

—*Network systems manager, 46*

The eyes, her voice, and her body language are the biggest turn ons. The biggest turn offs are attitudes that belittle other people.

—*Emergency medical technician, 35*

Most: when we have developed a thing that is uniquely ours and she appreciates it. Least: too many to list. All start with dishonesty.

—*Outdoor/rafting guide, 38*

THE

THING THAT

TURNS ME

ON MOST/

TURNS ME

OFF MOST

ABOUT A

Woman

IS...

THE SEXIEST THING A *Woman* CAN WEAR IN PRIVATE IS...

A little teddy with a thong (love thongs).
—*Dentist, 45*

Demure: one of my dress shirts that I wore that day or the day before and nothing else. Trashy: black bra and garter belt (or merry widow), black thong, seamed stockings, and black heels.
—*Art director, 33*

Something to take off...unhook, unzip, lift up, pull down.
—*Electrical engineer, 45*

THE

SEXIEST

THING A

Woman

CAN WEAR

IN PRIVATE

IS...

Pink lingerie and pigtails.
—*Stockbroker, 28*

A teddy, a tight t-shirt, a robe, a towel, a sweater, a coat, a blanket, a newspaper; all of the above, none of the above.
— *Psychologist, 40*

A silk pajama outfit (how corny, I know).
—*Teacher, 41*

I have no one desire here. It could be latex, leather, silk, or lace; bra; thong; garters; panties (crotchless at times). I love shiny things like lamés and metallics. Sometimes a skimpy and most revealing look is terrific, other times, fully clothed; sometimes a semi-see-through robe and the hot look underneath, but you can barely see it. They're all great.
—*Self-employed, 49*

It's not what she wears, it's how she wears it...attitude.
—*Firefighter, 26*

Filmy things; the kinds of things women wore in 1950s girlie magazines. (Talk about fixations; check my age.)

—*Retired advertising executive, 61*

...nothing or my shirt.

—*Outdoor/rafting guide, 38*

Lingerie. I know that is a typical male answer, but you asked.

—*Realtor, 37*

T-shirt and panties! That drives me wild!

—*Carpenter, 30*

I'm a notorious blouse peeker. Voyeurism, seeing something you're not supposed to. A woman who provides opportunities for me to peek, and appears unconscious of it, turns me on.

—*Retail manager, 37*

Scintillating statistics:

230 men said:
nothing/smile 46 times
stockings/garters/thigh
highs 38 times
bra/panties 38 times
(thongs, 14 times)
t-shirt 25 times
sheer/silk 23 times
lace 17 times
teddy 15 times
man's shirt 14 times

THE SEXIEST THING A *Woman* CAN WEAR IN PRIVATE IS...

THE

SEXIEST

THING A

Woman

CAN WEAR

IN PRIVATE

IS...

Nothing at all. I'm not into lingerie and I think the concepts of intrigue and mystery are overrated. There is nothing more beautiful than the naked body of the woman you love.

—*Engineer, 34*

Pure silk.

—*Psychologist, 44*

For me, something that would take hours to remove, lots of buttons and lace, and, yes, stockings.

—*Media consultant, 41*

Oversized white T-shirt, white socks, and a pretty smile.

—*Mail carrier, 43*

A long sleeved flannel shirt buttoned up halfway and the sleeves rolled halfway up her arms. The shirt is just long enough to hide her hips, but short enough to show off her shapely thighs. The top of the shirt is open enough to accentuate her cleavage, but not overtly showing off her breasts. It's simple and not gaudy.

—*Musician, 28*

I like accessories. Stockings are nice with garters and all. A woman with a tan looks terrific in white panties and bra. Maybe a nice lace shawl or something.

—*Business owner, 30*

Whatever makes her feel most sensual. Self-image goes a long way.

—*Writer, 37*

Tight denim shorts, with a loose-fitting man's dress shirt.

—*Regional account manager, 54*

THE

SEXIEST

THING A

Woman

CAN WEAR

IN PRIVATE

IS...

THE

SEXIEST

THING A

Woman

CAN WEAR

IN PRIVATE

IS...

Her smile, if it is sincere and honest. The twinkle in her eyes will complement the smile.

—*Contractor, 43*

Easy! Stockings (not hose, but thigh highs)! An obvious answer from a leg man, but there's something about stockings that make the leg look even better than when it's completely naked. Not to sell a frilly teddy or skimpy panties short, but nylon looks (and coincidentally feels) amazing clinging to a shapely leg. Those full-body nylon body-stockings were just the icing on the cake. But stockings…definitely. Oh yeah.

—*Advertising project manager, 26*

I love lingerie…but on a really cold night, how about a nice warm nightgown? I think that it depends on the mood of both of us. Sexy is loving each other.

—*Industrial supplier, 40*

Men's silk boxers and nothing else.

—*Businessman, 46*

To wear nothing at all. If she has to wear clothing, I guess it is the typical bra, panties, garter belt, and stockings. I do not like sleazy stuff, though…must be styled in a classy way.

—*House additions designer, 47*

Revealing white cotton panties under a black miniskirt.

—*Military serviceman, 33*

Leather.

—*Chemist, 29*

Lace undies and heels.

—*Computer consultant, 46*

THE

SEXIEST

THING A

Woman

CAN WEAR

IN PRIVATE

IS…

Part Three

THE

RELATIONSHIP

WHEN A *Woman* STAYS ON MY MIND, IT'S BECAUSE...

I am attracted to her appearance and personality, or either of the two. Laughter can get your head spinning for days.
—*Environmental activist, 37*

Extraordinary sex or rapport.
—*Slot machine technician, 43*

I feel good and valued after I have been with her.
—*Real estate appraiser, 38*

WHEN A

Woman

STAYS

ON MY

MIND, IT'S

BECAUSE...

She has touched my soul. She accepts me as me and finds that just dandy, thank you.

—*Salesman, 52*

I want to find out more. I love the way she looks, smells, tastes, excites me, enjoys my company, etc.

—*Martial arts instructor, 44*

I have had the desire to have or have had a sexual relationship.

—*Retired, 72*

There is something special about her that catches my attention. The other day I met a lady at Walmart. The way she communicated and carried herself interested me. She was not a super model, a little overweight, but she was a beautiful lady in the way she presented herself.

—*Lab technician, 31*

An electric moment, "the spark."

—*Caterer, 48*

She treats you with love and kindness. Great sex.
—*Accountant, 42*

She is a complete person with her own life/dreams/ambitions and she appears genuine—a rare female quality.

🍃 *Follow-up: How so about the genuineness?*

I often get a sense, when I am talking with a woman, that she has to think too long about her answers. It's not that she is necessarily being dishonest, it's just that she is choosing to measure and compose what she is willing to share. If I ask someone a question, I want her to answer me in as open and honest a fashion as possible. Nothing contrived. It is not an easy thing to pin down. It is just a sense you get that this person has nothing to hide and is not trying to impress you. She is simply relaying herself to you. It is a very refreshing experience.

—*Outdoor/rafting guide, 38*

WHEN A *Woman* STAYS ON MY MIND, IT'S BECAUSE...

69

WHEN A

Woman

STAYS

ON MY

MIND, IT'S

BECAUSE...

It's not looks, it's a quick second glance and you know if she's sexy or not.

—*Construction worker, 31*

She has touched me on a very deep level...and my mind can't let go of the possibilities.

—*Teacher, 34*

She has paid even a little bit of attention to me. That is where women have the advantage.

—*Disc jockey, 29*

What I find interesting in her mind and body. I would be lying if I said I didn't find her body exciting and I smile the whole day just thinking of the night before.

—*Truck driver, 31*

I like her and miss her.

—*Optician, 44*

She is really nice and/or is really attractive.

—*Firefighter, 35*

Her opinions intrigued me.

—*Website designer, 41*

When last we spoke/were together, something she did or said just struck me and gave me a rush. I'll be joking with a woman and she may say something coy or provocative that strikes a nerve and boom, my mind will replay that moment, AND that rush, all day long.

—*Advertising project manager, 26*

She's done something that really sets her apart from other people—whether it has anything to do with me or not is inconsequential—some act that shows her to have a character of true quality.

—*Chiropractor, 48*

The memory of a smile or a kind word or deed. Sometimes it's a particular song or certain scenery that triggers a memory.

—*Warehouse manager, 41*

WHEN A *Woman* STAYS ON MY MIND, IT'S BECAUSE...

WHEN A

Woman

STAYS

ON MY

MIND, IT'S

BECAUSE...

I can't wait to see her again, tell her my secrets, etc.
—*Engineer, 40*

The conversations on the phone, or in person, become really comfortable and filled with laughter.

☙ *Follow-up: Laughter is mentioned a lot—just how seductive is a good sense of humor?*

I find that body language, eye contact, and physical attraction seem to be heightened up a notch whenever there is genuine laughter between a couple. I think this is because an intimate bond is being created; you are each sharing a part of yourself. When the laughter slowly faded away in my ten-year marriage, it was a signal that we were no longer happy or entirely comfortable with each other.
—*Certified public accountant, 33*

I can't have her.
—*Truck driver, 41*

She is someone very special to me and probably great in bed.

—*Business owner, 44*

She has affected me in some way. Of course, there is always the physical attraction, but as I get older, I find that she must be complete (appearance, intelligence, a caring nature).

—*Government employee, 32*

She is fun to be around, a pleasant person, makes me laugh, we enjoy doing the same types of things, treats me with respect as a person.

—*Training manager, 40*

There have been shared intimate moments...without sex... and good communication... and chemistry.

—*Art director, 43*

WHEN A *Woman* STAYS ON MY MIND, IT'S BECAUSE...

I FEEL CLOSEST TO A *Woman* WHEN...

I feel that she loves me and is happy to be with me and I with her. And she walks up to me in front of the whole world, puts her arms around me, tells me she loves me, and gives me a nice big kiss on the lips.
—*Property management, 29*

We're just having laughs and quirky fun.
—*Contractor, 51*

She just lets it all hang out. She doesn't worry about being proper, or politically correct, or how her makeup is on, or anything else. She can just go for it, take some risks, and share the adventures with me!
—*Financial planner, 35*

I FEEL

CLOSEST

TO A

Woman

WHEN...

She's watching my back and she is looking out for me and my best interests, as I am with her.
—*Student, 25*

We are lying naked on a sofa in front of a fireplace on an October afternoon, listening to a rebroadcast of Orson Welles' *War of the Worlds*. At least that's what I was doing when I felt closest to a woman.
—*Retired advertising executive, 61*

I honestly never have.
—*Architect, 33*

She's being playful. Women grow up much faster than men, who, of course, don't grow up at all.
—*Events producer, 34*

I feel that I can trust her with every thought and feeling.

—*Film editor, 26*

When she says, "Let me pay this time."

—*Psychologist, 40*

We are enjoying doing everyday things, i.e., shopping, movies…

—*Field engineer, 29*

She can understand where I am coming from, has walked a mile in my shoes.

—*Truck driver, 31*

We are communicating as best friends, not based only on our attraction.

—*Geologist, 44*

When she opens up and is honest with me.

—*Military serviceman, 27*

I FEEL

CLOSEST

TO A

Woman

WHEN…

I FEEL

CLOSEST

TO A

Woman

WHEN...

I share my life with her.

—*Accountant, 59*

We have just made love.

—*Project manager, 36*

She needs me for comfort, understanding, and love.

—*Regional account manager, 53*

When there is mutual respect, admiration, and desire between both of us.

—*Salesman, 27*

Knows what I am thinking before I do.

—*Military serviceman, 33*

She is being herself.

—*Corporate manager, 41*

She looks at me as if she wouldn't want to be anywhere else.

—*Salesman, 34*

We share the same outlook on life.

—*Market researcher, 29*

She is honest with me, and doesn't try too hard to please me. She has her own sense of self.

—*Training manager, 41*

…she needs me and I need her.

—*Business owner, 51*

When I feel her presence inside me.

—*Website designer, 36*

She goes out of her way to make a good impression on my family and friends; when I am proud of who she is; when she makes me feel special; when we share memories that she helped make.

—*Slot machine technician, 43*

When she makes me feel good about myself.

—*Self-employed, 41*

I FEEL

CLOSEST

TO A

Woman

WHEN…

We are naked on a beach blanket with warm breezes on our bodies and a zillion stars twinkling.
—*Industrial supplier, 39*

We can talk endlessly.
—*Administrator, 47*

It's a lot of what people call chemistry, I guess.
—*Advertising project manager, 26*

...sitting together watching TV.
—*Musician, 27*

I FEEL

CLOSEST

TO A

Woman

WHEN...

MY THOUGHTS ON FALLING IN *Love...*

Done it...lost it...falling in love is a lot like falling out of an airplane—unless you have a parachute you are going to break your neck.

—*Military serviceman, 39*

I question if it really happens, at least in my life, it has been temporary. That, plus men are always associating it with sex——makes me wonder.

—*Writer, 41*

Do not believe women can fall in love…what they call love is most often lust blindness…dressed up as love to soothe their consciences. I do not believe men can fall in love, because they respond to hormonal urges and dress it up as love to fool the female target of opportunity they happen to be after.
—*Retired military serviceman, 64*

MY

THOUGHTS

ON FALLING

IN *Love…*

Never thought it was possible until recently…now I know it is the greatest thing that can ever happen to you. All the lousy relationships I have ever had only made me appreciate the real thing that much more.
—*Carpenter, 30*

When you find the right one she will knock you out with just a look. You have no control over this.
—*Basketball coach, 39*

I am too old for this…sigh…I can see a young woman turn the corner on a cold November day, and the wind will catch her hair just so, and she will have a slight pout to her mouth, and I will think, "Yes," to the beauty, the moment…the instant that is forever instantly lost, yet remains indelibly stamped on the corridors of memory. Falling in love, I think, is remembering the delight in the moment of recognizing someone whom you may never know, touch, or revel in, but captured nonetheless.

—*Counselor, 48*

Loss of independence.

—*Stockbroker, 28*

The feelings of commitment, acceptance, and newness really are exciting. Unfortunately, most people are putting their best foot forward in the early part of a relationship. They are what they would like to be rather than who they are. So, like when you buy a new car and drive off the lot, you are thinking this is the best thing ever. After twenty thousand miles and six months, it is just transportation; forty thousand miles and one year, the new car smell is gone and you find out what you really bought requires high maintenance and rarely ever works.

—*Self-employed, 38*

MY THOUGHTS ON FALLING IN *Love…*

MY

THOUGHTS

ON FALLING

IN *Love...*

It is a trap produced by women. Utterly indefinable.

—*Systems engineer, 32*

Sometimes it appears unattainable. It's amazing, but it seems to me that we rarely seem to get together with the one we really love. Something always seems to get in the way. Instead, we wind up settling for less and then regretting it until the end of our days or until two lawyers stumble upon the cash cow.

—*Teacher, 50*

I do not think I have ever truly fallen in love with a woman, even though I thought I had with my ex-wife.

🖎 *Follow-up: What makes you think you haven't?*

I have yet to be with a woman who is more important to me than anything else in my life—someone with whom I could do anything and be happy just because I am with her. A woman who shares my passion for life and many of my interests and who I look forward to seeing again as soon as we are apart, a woman without whom I truly cannot live.

—*Information director, 32*

Produces highly addictive brain chemicals. Makes one adolescent, for good and ill. Going too long without the sensation has damaging side effects. Next to parenthood, the most exalted human state.

—*Financial consultant, 48*

It can be great when it happens, but I'm not sure men, or is it just me, even know when it does.

—*Advertising project manager, 26*

Falling in love is easy. Staying in love is hard. And usually once you have mastered that, your partner has left and it is time to get over love, which is the hardest trick of all.

—*Computer technical support rep, 29*

They should bottle that feeling! The tough part is separating the great sex from the rest of it. What really is true love?

—*Financial planner, 35*

MY

THOUGHTS

ON FALLING

IN *Love...*

My

THOUGHTS

ON FALLING

IN *Love...*

...Sorry, but I've always gotten squashed like a bug on a headlight.

—*Business owner, 51*

It happens when you least expect it, and often with someone you wouldn't pick from a group, but there is a "click," meaning you and she just connect.

—*Attorney, 53*

Totally different from falling in lust or letting one's passions rule. To want to have the other person happy and content even if it means less for you. That is love.

—*Human resources manager, 37*

...overrated and women do it too easily.

—*Software engineer, 41*

The best time in the relationship, truly a natural high which you try to duplicate during the remainder of the relationship. When your patience wears out, then you break apart.

—*Certified public accountant, 54*

Anything more than a weekend makes my head hurt.

—*Stockbroker, 28*

It's wonderful, lovely, great for my heart, but let's not lose ourselves. True relationships take much, much more than love.

—*Entrepreneur, 47*

It is possible men love differently than women. Problems arise when a woman thinks a man should love her, her way, her style.

❧ *Follow-up: How so?*

A lot of men show their love through actions, not with words or by remembering dates or what was done on the first date—but I think the biggest difference is in the sex department. A woman may be emotionally tied to a man because they have sex. She gives herself to him. A man can have sex with a woman and not have any emotional ties at all (surprise, surprise!!). He just likes sex. I think sex is a lot better for a man with a woman for whom he has

MY THOUGHTS ON FALLING IN *Love...*

feelings, but I don't think a man has to have the emotional connection that most women do.

—*Supervisor, 47*

Falling in love is wonderful, but also scary. The next time she will have to be my best friend also.

—*Private investigator, 46*

MY

THOUGHTS

ON FALLING

IN *Love...*

I am trying to break up with a lady friend of one-and-a-half years who's so much in love with me, it's choking the life out of me. She has lots of $$$$, sex is good, wants it all the time, anywhere, will try most anything with me, and she is a very nice looking lady, and it seems so stupid of me to not love her back, but I can't.

—*Plumber, 35*

Falling in love and being in love are two different things...the first one's a drug and the second one's a cure.

—*Events producer, 34*

When you can have an actual conversation about something deep, rather than small talk. You love her mind as well as her body.

—*Self-employed, 28*

Not ready for that again, yet.

—*Architect, 33*

It definitely gets harder for both sexes as you get older and youthful optimism is tempered/dashed by the harsh realities of failed relationships and broken promises.

—*Outdoor/rafting guide, 38*

Never been there that I am aware of—have been in lust a few times and have been infatuated many times—but true love—ahhhhhh what is that like?

—*Writer, 51*

Makes you smile all the time, lose weight without trying…

—*Attorney, 45*

MY

THOUGHTS

ON FALLING

IN *Love…*

When I don't have it, it occupies my mind constantly.

—*Teacher, 35*

MY

THOUGHTS

ON FALLING

IN *Love...*

I

MARRIED MY *Wife* BECAUSE...

She was my best friend. There was an instant uniting of souls.

—Electronic engineer, 48

I liked her. Her children needed a father figure to help curb their increasingly unacceptable behavior. We were both tired of fighting the world alone. We wanted/needed each other.

—Business owner, 48

I

MARRIED

MY *Wife*

BECAUSE...

She captivated me from the first time I saw her. I just wanted to put my arms around her and never let go. We talked about everything. I thought that we were a perfect match.

—*Human resources manager, 38*

I've been married (and divorced) twice, so my reasons for marriage really should be taken with a grain of salt. The first time was pathetic. I kept trying to break up with the girl, but each time I did, I found her waiting for me in front of my home, crying and begging me to get back together. I really don't like hurting anyone, so in spite of my better judgment, we got back together—again and again. After eleven years of a hellish marriage, we were divorced. Seven years later, I married a coworker in the school where I teach. We got married for all the right reasons, companionship, good sex life, eye on the future, etc. The one item that was missing was compromise....When her youngest left for college, I got served with papers. Like I say, ask someone else! Not my area of expertise.

—*Teacher, 50*

Pure stupidity. If I had known then what I know now, I would not even have asked her out. No matter how much my friend urged me to do it.

—*Lab technician, 31*

She was adventurous, beautiful, and ambitious. We had an incredible time together and have a beautiful daughter from that time together. I still think that she is a great lady, but we just fell out of love. The woman I've loved the most, I didn't marry.

—*Laser salesman, 37*

No other woman I have ever known has made me feel so whole…everything about my fiancée is perfect (she'll tell you different though!). She is the first woman I have ever been involved with who didn't need a man, she wanted one! She is forever doing little things to show me how important I am to her. (How many women get up in the morning two hours before they have to in order to fix their boyfriend/husband lunch because they want to, not because they were asked to?) She is beautiful, intelligent, strong, independent, but still emotionally avail-

I

MARRIED

MY *Wife*

BECAUSE…

I

MARRIED

MY *Wife*

BECAUSE...

able. She is, simply put, all that, plus a side of chips! She is the answer to every prayer I have ever prayed and the fulfillment of every dream I have ever had! God, I love that woman!

—*Carpenter, 30*

I really wonder sometimes.

—*Salesman, 37*

In all honesty, we were kids and she was pregnant. It seemed the right thing to do at the time.

—*Military serviceman, 22*

The first time, I was very inexperienced and I married her because she seemed to like me. I know this sounds silly, but I took my second wife to a Jets game and when she started getting into it and hugging and high-fiving people, I was hooked.

—*Mail carrier, 42*

We laughed, talked, shared good times and bad, enjoyed each other's company outside and inside the bedroom.

—*Corporate administrator, 45*

A combination of reasons: intelligence, beauty, common sense, playfulness, and sexuality. Or: liquor, horniness, and her daddy had a shotgun.

—*Psychologist, 40*

I loved my first wife but I destroyed that relationship with unacceptable behavior. The second (and last ever) was an immediate replacement selected by the criteria that she was available, alive, and easy. (That was back in my drinking days—so I paid the penalty.)

—*Business owner, 46*

She made me feel like no other woman had before. I truly felt I could be myself and be 100 percent honest with her, and could do anything, even cry with her.

—*Military serviceman, 27*

I

MARRIED

MY *Wife*

BECAUSE...

I

MARRIED

MY *Wife*

BECAUSE...

I married my wives because they knocked me out. I've always had women in my life, but the ones that I couldn't stop thinking about, I just had to be with, ended up either as my wife or mistress.

—*Information director, 32*

Although I am divorced now, my original reason for marriage had a lot to do with how I felt the woman would be as a mother. I wanted children and wanted them to have a mother who was above all else, just exactly that. Someone who had an inner kindness and a gentle spirit. I was married eighteen years before divorcing.

—*Lumber broker, 43*

I was desperate. Seriously…I married at thirty-eight after I had reached my midlife crisis, I guess. I was tired of spending birthdays and holidays alone or with friends, so when she proposed to me, I accepted quickly. It was a mistake, and the next time I marry, it will be for entirely different reasons.

—*Bank officer, 44*

I was deeply in love with her.

—*Chiropractor, 48*

For love, i.e., belonging, understanding, touching, connecting.

—*Commercial driver, 29*

Great sex.

—*Teacher, 49*

I was ready to settle down and start a family.

—*Website designer, 34*

I thought we could be together for the long haul (boy was I wrong!).

—*Arbitrator, 37*

Compatibility.

—*Engineer, 43*

I MARRIED MY *Wife* BECAUSE...

I

MARRIED

MY *Wife*

BECAUSE...

I thought she was unique—different from all the rest, but funny, now the same things I considered in her to be unique, get on my nerves.

—*Engineer, 41*

First time: I was young, dumb, and horny. Second time: I was in love with her. Third time: she was more than my sexual equal. She loved sex even more than I do (couldn't keep up with her).

✎ *Follow-up: Any words of wisdom on the institution of marriage?*

I have married because I thought it was the thing to do (1st time), for love (2nd time), and for sex (3rd time). All I need now is a rich one. :-) But in all of the marriages, the one thing that was missing was complete honesty. I don't know why people think it is best to hide or keep things from their partners. It only causes trouble when the truth comes out (and the truth does come out, nine times out of ten).

—*Systems analyst, 51*

Low self-esteem…didn't think anyone would marry me.

—*Bioinformation specialist, 43*

I was young and thought I was in love. Felt that way for many years.…If I had it to do all over again, I wouldn't have gotten married.…The years have just hurt her and me.…We both feel very alone and isolated.

—*Warehouse manager, 41*

Everyone else was getting married and settling down.

—*Consultant, 41*

I am not married, but I have been in a relationship that is far and away, above all others. She knows me the best, laughs at my stupid jokes, and still tells me she loves me.

—*Supervisor, 37*

I MARRIED MY *Wife* BECAUSE…

I

MARRIED

MY *Wife*

BECAUSE...

Because I thought they saw more in me besides money and sex. I was wrong.

—*Military serviceman, 40*

The first time I looked into her eyes I knew immediately and absolutely we were going to be married. There was such sincerity and passion in those eyes.

—*Designer, 47*

I am single. However, I will know I have found my wife when I can stand to be around the woman at least 85 percent of the time and feel that warm and fuzzy feeling for at least 50 percent of the time.

—*Information systems analyst, 31*

She was the woman I wanted to be with for the rest of my life.

—*Computer technical support rep, 33*

She was very down-to-earth and had a natural desire to please me to no end. Her smile was radiating and you could feel her love!

—*Illustrator, 41*

Infidelity
HAPPENS
WHEN...

A lack of intimacy will almost always result in infidelity, and by intimacy I don't mean sex necessarily. I mean deep communication.
—*Law enforcement officer, 38*

The better the sex, the less probability of infidelity. Once in my life I had a partner that was so good that I never thought of straying because I didn't think that there could possibly be anyone out there as good. We're talking the kind of sex that you read about in a novel and think that the author must have a wild imagination because it couldn't be that good. Well, it

Infidelity

HAPPENS

WHEN...

was no dream, but it's gone. It lasted almost a year and I never wanted it to end. I nearly lost my meager mind when she left. I never cheated on that one. However, as a rule, even if the relationship is good and the sex is great, I think that there is an occasional desire to experience different. Different textures, shapes, fits, the unknown little surprises that you would never know without being with someone. Yes, I am a pig! Yes, trust is important in a relationship. No, I wouldn't like that if she did it to me. Yes, it makes me feel alive. Just maybe two or three times a year would be nice (would be, not is).
—*Military serviceman, 36*

Not the right partner.
—*Systems engineer, 45*

Almost invariably when I hear about the cliche of a man cheating on a woman, I find the underlying story much more complex than the woman would have you believe. Men don't cheat just because. They are driven to it by years of pain and unfulfilled expectations.

🖋 *Follow-up: Aren't there plenty of guys who are just skirt chasers...it wouldn't matter who they had at home?*

When a man is asking his partner to marry him, he wants a lifetime of romantic love and friendship. That is his dream. He is not thinking that this is a temporary situation....For this dream to die, it will take a great deal of disappointment....It is not something he wants to happen. Nobody (women included) wants their new-found love and accompanying commitment to fail.

—*Outdoor/rafting guide, 38*

I don't know. Neither does the married woman who I'm seeing now.

—*Computer consultant, 45*

Two reasons: first, it's like being mayor for a long time. In the normal course of the job, by simply making decisions, you eventually piss off every constituency you ever had. And you're voted out. In the normal course of marriage, you eventually touch

Infidelity
HAPPENS
WHEN...

103

every trigger your partner has, and it's over. Second, you reach a point in life where the future looks like it's going to be absolutely identical to the past, and since you're just a bit bored with the present, the prospect becomes bleak. The midlife crisis, and the steps toward divorce, begin.

—*Retired advertising executive, 61*

Infidelity

HAPPENS

WHEN...

Not feeling cared about. I admit it, men are children.

—*Pharmacist, 44*

I truly feel that if infidelity is taking place, then you're not with the one who was meant for you. So many people are just with someone to be with someone and didn't really hold out for a true love. If people really, really love each other on that higher plane, infidelity won't take place. There is way too much to lose.

—*Salesman, 37*

There are probably a hundred reasons men give and none of them make any sense to me.

—*Metal framer, 46*

The need to periodically fall in love. Crassly, the stimulation of "a bit of strange." Filling the holes in an incomplete relationship. Shoring up a wounded ego. Revenge. Risk. Boredom. Distraction. Escape. Oblivion. Fun.

—*Financial consultant, 48*

Falling out of love; who knows why? Love is a very elusive thing. It comes and it goes and there's no rational way of explaining it. It's glorious when it IS; it's a nightmare when it isn't.

—*Teacher, 50*

There is no excuse for it, even though I have been guilty of it. If people are unhappy in their present relationship and desire to be with another woman/man, they should end the relationship. Infidelity doesn't always have to be sexual. Emotional infidelity is as equally powerful, if not more.

—*Computer technical support rep, 35*

Infidelity

HAPPENS

WHEN...

105

I think it happens because people are looking for something they don't have in their current relationship, but are too chicken to deal with ending it before chasing another. It never works.

—*Arbitrator, 37*

An endless, ageless, unanswerable question that I suspect will continue to be a mystery for as long as the human species exists. For the sake of expediency, I will state the most obvious answer—man's continuous penchant for variety. Monogamous creatures we are not!!

❧ *Follow-up: So how come a lot of men are faithful?*

There are many faithful men who find infidelity distasteful for strong moral reasons, religious or otherwise. These men, in my opinion, value their family life, their overall sense of fairness, much more than a temporary sexual escapade. They weigh the risk of the possible harmful effect…and decide against it. I think the majority of men, faithful or unfaithful, eventually want and think about sexual encounters with

Infidelity

HAPPENS

WHEN…

a variety of women. Some act upon this desire, oth-ers don't.

—*Account representative, 33*

Arousal has no conscience.

—*Network engineer, 38*

You won't like my answer, but it would be OK for me but not for my partner.

❧ *Follow-up: How so?*

I should back up a little and tell you I wasn't always like this. Poor me :-(I've got a lot of bad memories about being faithful. I was raising the kids and run-ning a business while my ex was working and mak-ing a new life for herself that didn't include any of us. There's no excuse for the way I feel, but it's sort of like I missed out on something. I still have a sincere respect for (most) women and wouldn't think of hurting anyone, but I sure love sex...

—*Graphic artist, 61*

Infidelity
HAPPENS

WHEN...

107

Infidelity

HAPPENS

WHEN...

Men don't have to fall in love to have sex, unlike women. Men need sexual gratification more than women, it seems. If they don't get it at home then some will seek it elsewhere. This most often happens when the man's marriage lacks intimacy and the woman forgot how or doesn't want to make the man feel good about himself, or it's a marriage of convenience.

—*Self-employed, 41*

Men, I think, are always the hunter/gatherer (per Rob Becker in *Defending the Caveman*) and the hunting/gathering tends to extend to female "pelts" in addition to animal ones...it is a restating of "validity," "virility," "desire." What is it in women? I have no clue. I suspect, though, that the motives are somewhat different, not any more noble per se, just different.

—*Therapist, 48*

There is never, ever an excuse for infidelity. If you want to cheat on me, leave me first, then you can screw anybody your dark little heart desires. I have never cheated on anyone and I never intend to.

—*Healthcare provider, 26*

Been there! Done that! While I was too young and didn't realize how fortunate I was with whom I had. Animal instinct spurred me on to other "grassy fields."

—*Retired journalist, 67*

It stinks and is cruel. It is the most devastating breach of trust there is.

—*Market researcher, 38*

Infidelity

HAPPENS

WHEN...

I KNEW THE *marriage* WAS OVER WHEN...

When my wife told me it was over, after thirty years. She said, "We have no interests in common." Hard to swallow at first, but true. I took the initiative on the divorce and the past seven years have been the best of my life—just me and m' dog. Many friends, male and female, to be sure, but I also love my solitude.

—*Writer, 67*

When I decided that I didn't care enough to go the extra distance for her.

—*Landscaper, 31*

I
KNEW THE
marriage
WAS OVER
WHEN...

I would rather stay at work than go home to see my wife. I would look at her and feel nothing romantically. I remember going to some garage sales with her and watching her walk down the street and thinking that I would not turn my head to look at her if I did not know who she was. I realized that I had married the wrong woman. I needed to be married to a woman who would turn my head.

—*Information director, 32*

On the day I went to an ATM to make a withdrawal and I found out all of our accounts had been closed five days prior. I should have known something was up—she initiated having sex more in those four nights prior to discovery than she had in the last four years of our marriage.

—*Caterer, 48*

Groucho Marx once said, "I'd never join a club that would have me as a member." I think that was what went wrong with my second marriage. For six years we had a wonderful, noncommittal, incredibly sexy relationship. But once I committed, she began to withdraw. It was like she felt, "If he's so desperate he'd ask to marry me, I don't want anything to do with him." The marriage lasted just a few months.

—*Retired advertising executive, 61*

We were both lonely, even when we were together, and we began to live separate lives. We no longer felt any connection to each other, except for the kids. I only realize that now in retrospect. (She asked for the divorce.)

—*Certified public accountant, 33*

She started telling me she never truly loved me. That really hurt a lot.

—*Computer technical support rep, 37*

Hmm…probably, if I am to be honest, within one year after we were married…(it lasted twenty-three years…sad huh?).

🖎 *Follow-up: Why did your marriage last as long as it did?*

I KNEW THE *marriage* WAS OVER WHEN…

I

KNEW THE

marriage

WAS OVER

WHEN...

First, we had five terrific children, and we were a great mom and dad to them. Three were born in our first two-and-a-half years of marriage, so the cement was set very quickly. We were just too darn busy to concern ourselves with our relationship in any personal, one-on-one way. The other reason is more abstract. In short, it is that we never thought divorce was an option. Come hell or high water, we would stay together. In our twenty-third year, there came a point when I told her I was going to move out and separate, and she shocked me by saying, "Why don't I just go down to the lawyer and fill out the divorce papers?" She was obviously as ready as I was!
—*Salesman, 51*

She tried to change me and I rebelled.

☙ *Follow-up: Was it that you didn't agree with the changes as being right for you, or, rather, just the idea that someone was trying to change you?*

When someone loves you she should accept the fact that we all have unique habits. Just because you get married, it does not mean you can change those habits or that you should even try to do that. When I got married I was playing ball six days a week, and, after marriage, never again. That was the beginning of the end right away, but we managed to stay together for eight years.

—*Systems analyst, 34*

There were periods in my marriage when we did not make love for two or three years. I am even embarrassed to say that (sorry, but tears are filling up my bottom eyelid). There were times in my marriage when I even had to make appointments to make love. But when my wife started to masturbate me to relieve my desire, I knew it was over. Please keep in mind that this was not the only reason my marriage fell apart, but one of them.

—*Business owner, 49*

She got pregnant by another man.

—*Electronic repairman, 48*

I KNEW THE *marriage* WAS OVER WHEN...

115

I

KNEW THE

marriage

WAS OVER

WHEN...

When it was common for one of us to sleep on the couch and intimacy felt like a chore rather than fun.
—*Military serviceman, 27*

My wife's work was more important than our marriage.
—*Chiropractor, 48*

She began exhibiting characteristics of her mother, whom I hate now as much as she hated me then. She also started trashing me privately with my oldest daughter and with our friends at Sunday school. I have no friends left in Nashville anymore.
—*Warehouse manager, 41*

I was happier when she was away.
—*Carpenter, 30*

I caught her in a bold-faced lie and when a male stranger started calling her. I answered the phone one time and he asked to speak with her, so I said, "Hey, it's your boyfriend!" Then she grabbed the phone and hit me over the head with it, which my kids witnessed. I saw stars but did not retaliate. I'm proud to say that I've never hit a woman.

—*Optician, 48*

She took back a promise she said she never would.

—*Commercial driver, 29*

She started dating another woman.

—*Arbitrator, 37*

When I began to wish I were dead instead. Of course I didn't really wish this, but in trying to figure out how to find happiness again, it seemed the only way was to get out of the marriage. And it also seemed like the only way to get out without hurting a ton of people was to be dead. That didn't happen and in the end I had to find my happiness. So I got out. I'm still not entirely happy, but I can look at the man in the mirror without flinching. I think I made the right decision.

—*Government employee, 37*

I KNEW THE *marriage* WAS OVER WHEN...

I

KNEW THE

marriage

WAS OVER

WHEN...

We could both walk away from each other and not feel anything inside.

—*Supervisor, 41*

It was fortunately…and it was when she said she did not want to work on it, or change, or work on herself.

—*Insurance, 37*

My wife told me I could not have another chance.

—*Self-employed, 43*

She did not want my kids from another marriage, who live with me.

—*Dentist, 45*

She got fat, cheated on me, and lost interest in sex.

—*Systems analyst, 30*

I kept looking for an affair.

—*Project manager, 35*

When she didn't seem to care about life anymore. I just wanted out. I didn't care how. She didn't want to work, she didn't want to cook, clean, or do laundry. She didn't want to shower and fix herself up, so I guess I married a channel surfer and professional complainer. If I only knew she was going to turn out that way, I would never have married her. I tried counseling and tried talking to her about it, to no avail. So I gave her everything and asked her to leave.

—*Operations manager, 37*

We had never really worked on our "non-negotiables." The big one was that she desperately wanted kids before her biological clock ran out. I was avoiding the issue at the time. It became a major concern, but we never really fought. I just lost interest, I suppose. We went our separate ways and she still calls to say hello once in a while.

—*Geologist, 44*

I KNEW THE *marriage* WAS OVER WHEN...

I KNEW THE *marriage* WAS OVER WHEN...

After twenty-three years together, my wife was diagnosed with a rapid type of cancer and she died eleven months later. She was sweet, kind, beautiful, and a wonderful wife and mother. She was forty-four years old when she died. I have no doubt that had she lived we would have finished raising our children together, shared some wonderful retirement years, and enjoyed old age together. I have one thought to add at this point for anyone who reads this. If you are in a good relationship with a person whom you love and respect, please, please, don't take that person or the beauty of that relationship lightly or for granted. Hold that person and tell her how wonderful she is and how much you love her and what an important part of your life she is, early on, each and every day. There will come a day, for one of you, when that person is no longer there to hear those things. Don't leave them unsaid.

—*Retired commercial pilot, 53*

Part Four

HEAVY

BREATHING

WHAT MAKES *sex* GOOD, REALLY GOOD?

When you just do it. No planning. No rules. Anything goes.

—*Construction worker, 31*

A wanting of the other. Technique does not matter. Acrobatics and experimentalism do not matter. To burn in one another's presence matters.

—*Writer, 37*

The emotional connection, first and foremost. After that, a woman who is aggressive in bed....My dad used to say all men want a lady on their arm and a slut in their bed...I agree.

—*Carpenter, 30*

To love the right person is like having all the wealth at your feet. To make love to the right person is like being reborn over and over again.

—*Supervisor, 45*

Good sex is when she is looking great and is also turned on by me. Great sex is all of the above, plus love.

—*Salesman, 28*

Total exposure of oneself and total giving.

—*Real estate broker, 45*

There are two types of great sex. 1) When there is love and emotion and you look into each other's eyes and feel the love between the two of you. The candles, the soft music, and maybe some rose petals.

WHAT MAKES *sex* GOOD, REALLY GOOD?

2) Really hot steamy sex when you can't get out of your clothes fast enough and it doesn't matter where the two of you are or the time of day. In short, I guess it is just how the other partner makes you feel.

—*Small business owner, 30*

There has to be an intense mixture of desire, passion, and trust for the sex to be good enough to scramble the brain.

—*Computer technical support rep, 27*

A partner who participates. I have to say that for all the complaining I hear from women about how lousy men are in bed, 75 percent of the lovers I've had over the years have thought that the woman's role during sex is to lie there. Enthusiasm is very sexy, believe it or not (and not fake enthusiasm either—we know when you do that, by the way, we're not idiots. OK, maybe we are, but not as much as you think).

—*Events producer, 34*

WHAT

MAKES

sex

GOOD,

REALLY

GOOD?

WHAT

MAKES

Sex

GOOD,

REALLY

GOOD?

Letting your inhibitions go! Being comfortable with your body and willing to share with your partner.
—*Financial planner, 35*

Deep love, intense intimacy, time, patience, exploration, freedom, lack of inhibitions, and deriving most of your own pleasure from the pleasure of your partner.
—*Chiropractor, 48*

It's going to sound corny, but it's love that makes sex special and gives you the bells and whistles with the fireworks.
—*Network engineer, 38*

Communication!
—*Military serviceman, 33*

The other party really, fully cooperating, showing that she truly wants to be there, doing what she's doing.
—*Building contractor, 47*

When the woman is sexual and feminine during the day, and foreplay and playfulness take place anytime, anywhere. The way she dresses, touches, smells, and enjoys having me aroused. The actual sex act is not the ultimate, it's the above and more. Verbal playfulness and erotica are very nice, too! Some exhibitionist tendencies can be fun or verbal exchange of fantasies. Oh—it's important that a woman really likes to get dirty sometimes, as well as to be made tender love to. This is important to a man.

—*Career coach, 53*

When a woman acts out her feelings in a decisive way in bed. Don't hold back. Don't play the proverbial angel in a white dress. You know there's a way of letting a man know what you want without being too much the "tramp." Most of the women (not all) I have gone to bed with, I have known for a really long time. I don't advocate jumping into bed. It accomplishes nothing. And it can be very destructive to a beginning relationship.

—*Optician, 52*

WHAT

MAKES

sex

GOOD,

REALLY

GOOD?

WHAT MAKES *sex* GOOD, REALLY GOOD?

I know it's a cliché, but when she is genuine and honest, that's really all it takes.

—*Outdoor/rafting guide, 38*

It satisfies an urge that seems to have an existence of its own.

—*Teacher, 50*

Nothing makes it better than being with someone you really care about. But, going on the fact that I have not been in love with everyone I have slept with, being with someone who is very expressive and physical.

—*Pharmacist, 30*

Just being with the right woman is as good as it can get.

—*Military serviceman, 22*

When you haven't had it for a while.

—*Self-employed, 27*

The six inches between your or her ears and how well emotionally and intellectually you are connected.

—*Salesman, 44*

I have always found that a woman who maintains eye contact with me while pleasuring me, or herself, is erotic. I have found women who naturally do this and sex was very, very good. Even when everything else turned out to be wrong, as with my ex-wife (#2), this eye-contact thing remains with me.

—*Retired advertising executive, 61*

Educating oneself, and practicing what one has learned.

—*Salesman, 51*

Chemistry! And it's either there or it's not.

—*Professional speaker, 38*

Trust and openness. Enough said.

—*Film editor, 26*

WHAT

MAKES

sex

GOOD,

REALLY

GOOD?

WHAT

MAKES

sex

GOOD,

REALLY

GOOD?

The intimacy, the caring and secure feeling, the relief.
—*Insurance salesman, 36*

Anticipation…taking your time…massage (running your fingers across the skin or with massage oil).
—*Engineer, 48*

Someone I'm in love with and feel close to and someone who truly loves sex…makes me feel like I'm really satisfying her.
—*Financial analyst, 37*

Passion, undiluted passion. Let it all go. Get down and get dirty!
—*Builder, 39*

Ability to share and freedom to experience any and all sensations that feel good. Exploring the unexpected. Surprises. Good sexy talk.
—*Martial arts instructor, 44*

Nice and slow!
—*Realtor, 54*

I think it is two people who truly want to do everything they can to completely satisfy their partner. You get to know what your partner likes and doesn't like and you do and don't do those exact things. Of course, you have to keep it spicy, and avoid a routine, but, basically, what we like today is what we are going to like tomorrow, as well… so you do have to never lose touch with the basics.

—*Government employee, 37*

Knowing the woman and being friends first.

—*Network engineer, 31*

When there is that deep connection and a compatibility in level of passion, openness, mutuality, intimacy, and trust. Physical attraction.

🖎 *Follow-up: How come so many guys like to just pile on the numbers?*

It's very difficult to answer your question without talking about gender role stereotypes. Most men who trumpet their conquest from the highest mountain top are living up to a certain stereotype

WHAT

MAKES

sex

GOOD,

REALLY

GOOD?

131

WHAT MAKES *sex* GOOD, REALLY GOOD?

about what it is to be a man. I believe that the men who took the time to give you thoughtful answers about what makes sex good are not typically bragging about their conquests. I think that these are, for the most part, two different groups of men.

—*Teacher, 35*

It is playful.

—*Arbitrator, 38*

Kissing—WHAT I LIKE MOST/DISLIKE... WHAT'S THE BEST/WORST...

Like most: intense, sensual, knowing the woman is "there" 100 percent. Dislike most? Anything less.
—*Property manager, 41*

Just long, slow and soft, with nice tongue teasing.

Follow-up: Describe a great kiss.

Tenderly enter the mouth, touch and tease, don't try to overwhelm, at least not at first, later on...well that may be different. I like to touch gently, and move my lips on hers, just a little bit now, not 7.5 on the Richter Scale. Women I know sometimes seem to

Kissing—

WHAT I

LIKE MOST/

DISLIKE...

WHAT'S

THE BEST/

WORST...

want to drive their tongue to your tonsils. To me, kissing is a gentle thing—to feel the lips and warmth of the woman, to explore the feelings of desire in a slow and easy way. Patience in all things is good advice and I think it applies to kissing also. Take your time, enjoy the experience, and linger a while there. <smile>

—*Stockbroker, 28*

A wet tongue that slides across the lips and neck.
—*Construction worker, 31*

Worst was a young lady that wore bad tasting lipstick, and another who had a shaved top lip.

🕭 *Follow-up: Describe a great kiss.*

A kiss should start gently, not too wet or too dry, and with the mouth just slightly open. Tilting your head a little, lightly press your lips just off center to hers, again and again, each time turning your head to the left and then to the right, and each kiss lasting longer and longer. As you become more passionate, the kisses become more wet with hers, your tongue probing into her mouth. With your mouth more open, sensually run your tongue down her neck, kissing your way back up to her ear, touching her face ever so lightly with the back of your fingers, then caressing her head.

—*Photographer, 45*

Like most: to have my lips enveloped by a woman's mouth. Lipstick is erotic. Having a woman open herself to you in a kiss, where one can feel the desire. Dislike most: a closed kiss, where you have to pry the emotions out of her. Best kiss: a woman, in the process of divorce after a loveless marriage of eight years, who placed her mouth on mine and through her lips and tongue, expressed all the loneliness, longing, desire, and pain of not having been intimate with anyone for so long.

—*Financial planner, 37*

The best is playfulness—each person giving and taking. I dislike a woman who shoves her tongue in my mouth and just sits it there.

—*Accountant, 38*

Kissing—

WHAT I

LIKE MOST/

DISLIKE...

WHAT'S

THE BEST/

WORST...

135

Kissing—

WHAT I

LIKE MOST/

DISLIKE...

WHAT'S

THE BEST/

WORST...

Best ever—I met a woman online a few years ago. We talked online and later on the phone for about six months. We fell in love and didn't have any idea what each other looked like (this was before scanners were so prevalent and online pictures were somewhat rare). When we finally decided to get together, we agreed that we would meet at her apartment, I would knock on the door, we'd both close our eyes and she would take my hand and lead me to the couch. She sat beside me, both of us with our eyes still closed, and we kissed before we said a word. It was the most magical kiss of my life.

—*Corporate manager, 51*

Like most: when you feel the heat in the back of your partner's throat. Dislike most: when your partner seems to use kissing solely as foreplay. Best ever—ex-girlfriend, when we first met. Worst ever: ex-girlfriend, towards the end of our relationship.

—*Electrician, 33*

Best: a gentleman never tells, but, Jen, if you read this, I miss you. Worst: the first time I gave some tongue and the girl almost gagged.

—*Salesman, 29*

I like it most when she whimpers and goes limp in my arms; least, when she tries too hard to impress. Generally enjoy rubbing lips on and off…left and right grazing.

🍂 *Follow-up: What's left and right grazing?*

Short of a live demonstration, the best I can describe it is that I would use both my lips to draw circles, taking, between mine, her upper lip and moving my lips in a circular motion to the joint of her upper/lower lips, kissing the joint-corner repeatedly, then taking the lower lip between mine and continuing the trip to the other side where her lips join. I find that the motion of having one lip at a time captured between mine and rubbed as I travel its length, is very pleasant to the woman I'm kissing.

—*Teacher, 50*

Kissing—

WHAT I

LIKE MOST/

DISLIKE…

WHAT'S

THE BEST/

WORST…

137

Kissing—

WHAT I

LIKE MOST/

DISLIKE...

WHAT'S

THE BEST/

WORST...

Best: long, hard, wet, gasping for breath kind of passionate kisses that leave your jaw out of place when you're done. Worst: small pecks that make silly noises.

—*Film editor, 26*

My best almost made me climax in my jeans. My worst was like a sword fight with our tongues.

✒ *Follow-up: Describe a great kiss beginning to end.*

I guess it all starts with the chemistry developing between the man and woman. Before the lips even touch, the hearts must be in tune, sharing the same beat. The kiss is a transfer of all the passion and desire both bodies hold. Before it can become earth-shaking, the pressure must build, so it has to be slow and easy at first, then turn into a complete sharing of emotions. The lips should first touch gently and then part. If there is a spark, then a second gentle kiss, only with a longer stay. The big one starts with the mouths opening and the tongues lightly touching and dancing with each other softly, then deeper and deeper, until they are sharing each other's mouths. The lips get locked together as though they were creating a seal to stop any of the passion from escaping. Finally, when the body can't keep up with the passion that has been exchanged, the mouths part and a sigh is released.

—*Truck driver, 41*

The best kiss ever? At a Heart concert on July 4 with a special lady at the top of an open-air stadium. The band playing *Alone*…and fireworks (real and in our minds) blasting all over the horizon.

—*Webmaster, 39*

I like to kiss and be kissed until I am dizzy. To be kissed by a woman whose lips don't just meet yours, but surround yours, engulfing them, traveling across them, then exploring them, one at a time; having, in one fluid motion, the mouth caressed and the chin bitten; then traveling down to the neck, up to the ear, and lingering across the cheeks.

—*Art director, 37*

Kissing—

WHAT I

LIKE MOST/

DISLIKE…

WHAT'S

THE BEST/

WORST…

139

Kissing—

WHAT I

LIKE MOST/

DISLIKE...

WHAT'S

THE BEST/

WORST...

Best ever was a lovely lady I will call Ginger, in a frozen train car, huddled beneath a Hudson Bay blanket, between Fort Wayne and Chicago, some twenty-three years ago...hmmm...worst? I don't think I believe in worst, I suspect there are just degrees of "less best."

—*Therapist, 48*

The softer and moister the lips, the more lost I get in the moment.

—*Business owner, 34*

Like most: I love full lips that are used completely. Soft, yet firm. Long, but not smothering. Small gentle flicks of the tongue. Dislike: hard, brash attack. Best is when our mouths melt together and our tongues waltz without conscious thought....Worst is when it is restrained, nervous, self-conscious or really bad breath. Kissing after oral sex feels a bit strange, but I wouldn't want her to be insulted.

—*Slot machine technician, 43*

Continuing to circle and circle.

—*Pharmacist, 41*

Passionate kisses followed by hot breath in the face. Kissing behind the neck and the ears during love making.

—*Government employee, 38*

Best... my fiancée; you can feel the love and fire. Worst... smoker, disgusting!

—*Accountant, 42*

Dislike someone who opens their mouth too wide.

—*Truck driver, 30*

Kissing—

WHAT I

LIKE MOST/

DISLIKE...

WHAT'S

THE BEST/

WORST...

IT'S A LITTLE *kinky*, BUT I LOVE (OR WOULD LOVE)...

One night of ecstasy, where a harem of women use nothing but their tongues on me and all over, all night (I know this sounds so trite).
—*Film editor, 26*

A lesbian lover who shares her interest with me. If any guy answers anything else, he's lying!
—*Construction worker, 38*

To go to a swingers club with a woman. It does not matter whether we participate or not...I just want to go.
—*Financial planner, 46*

IT'S

A LITTLE

kinky, BUT

I LOVE

(OR WOULD

LOVE)...

This woman tied me up one night when we were both drunk. She blindfolded me and everything. I never expected it, but being completely helpless was absolutely wonderful. I have never done it again, but would like to try it some more.

—*Salesman, 30*

Getting "naughty" in public. Not so that we can be seen, but under a table in a dark restaurant, maybe in the men's room or someplace discreet. There is something really, really exciting about being out of the expected environment. It's not just the "might get caught" thing. It's the "we couldn't wait, we want each other right now" thing. Plus, I have a strange liking for fooling around fully clothed and just sorta reaching under and around and over. Guess that's more part of the "have to have you now" aspect. Whatever the case, that's just plain hot.

—*Advertising project manager, 26*

Would love to have a video of my love and myself having sex.

—*Retired state employee, 58*

Having sex in the same room as another couple—something very "high school" about it—and "dirty" too. Those are the things that make it exciting. Or having sex on the roof of a building in the afternoon. Or on a private beach. Or on a boat in the middle of a lake somewhere. But the excitement has to be shared by both partners or it wouldn't be nearly as much fun.

—*Attorney, 35*

I've pondered this one a while. I guess I'm more conventional than I sometimes imagine myself to be. I like good old fashioned straight sex. I especially like it with the woman on top, but nothing kinky really appeals to me. On the other hand, I'm open to suggestions and I'll try just about anything.

—*Teacher, 50*

To join the Mile High Club. The thought of making love to my fiancée on a crowded plane high above the Earth… mmmmm, mmmmm!

—*Carpenter, 30*

Scintillating statistics:

191 men mentioned:
threesomes 45 times
mild bondage/
domination 41 times
anal sex 37 times
oral sex 37 times
semi-public sex
31 times

IT'S

A LITTLE

kinky, BUT

I LOVE

(OR WOULD

LOVE)…

IT'S A LITTLE *kinky*, BUT I LOVE (OR WOULD LOVE)...

I love it when a woman is totally uninhibited when making love. By that I mean that she would let me do anything to her. This does not include hurting her or giving her any type of discomfort, of course, but, for example, running my tongue all over her body is the most erotic kind of lovemaking to me. To some people that might seem kinky, but to me it's my way of expressing my love, and there is nothing dirty about making love.

—*Computer technical support rep, 37*

That's a tough one to answer. It's all really good with the right partner and I don't look at things as being kinky.

—*Laser salesman, 38*

To try a threesome with two women at least once.

✎ *Follow-up: Are some fantasies maybe meant to remain just that, fantasies?*

If the opportunity arose, I'm really unsure what my reaction would be. I don't think I'd have a problem seeing my wife or girlfriend with another woman as long as I'm involved somehow. I don't think I could do this with a couple of strangers, though. I would have to know them both very well.

—*Website designer, 36*

To eat fresh strawberries and whipped cream from my lover's body, with champagne on the side, on a beach.

—*Corporate manager, 42*

There are a lot of things that I would love to try sexually even though they would be considered kinky by many people. I love anal stimulation. I have always had a fantasy about a woman with a strap-on dildo. It would be fun to have a woman be the one controlling the intercourse.

—*Information director, 32*

I love to play master and have a sex slave.

—*Printer, 48*

IT'S

A LITTLE

kinky, BUT

I LOVE

(OR WOULD

LOVE)...

IT'S

A LITTLE

kinky, BUT

I LOVE

(OR WOULD

LOVE)...

Having my lady arrive to go on a date wearing just her trench coat and a smile.

—*Teacher, 38*

I thoroughly love it when we each take turns (switch roles). Oftentimes, it is mild bondage and domination (mild spankings) when I am in charge. When my mate takes charge, it is most enjoyable for me when she uses her imagination and leaves me wondering. A woman who is spontaneous and totally unafraid of her sexuality is most sensuous of all.

—*Real estate broker, 45*

My thoughts on bringing a *Woman* to orgasm are...

The degree of arousal is really the whole story. Some people just fit together and it's great, some don't and it stinks.

—*Website designer, 36*

Foreplay is long and intense, with lots of teasing, exploring, and touching.

—*College instructor, 42*

From oral manipulation or massaging her G-spot...very seldom from intercourse itself.

—*Warehouse manager, 41*

MY

THOUGHTS

ON

BRINGING

A *Woman*

TO ORGASM

ARE...

Nothing compares to modern electronic toys for stimulating nerve endings. Especially when coupled with guided imagery helping her explore taboo fantasies. And most especially when preceded by a lot of attention to her skin and her mind. On the other hand, missionary position powered by intense feelings of love—just discovered or just rekindled—works damn well, too.

—*Financial consultant, 48*

You have discovered what turns her on, and are doing it. Wife #2, for example, liked a little rough stuff (although I never really fancied it myself, I gave her a bit of biting and slapping at her request).

—*Retired advertising executive, 61*

Depends. Some when they are on top. Most when they are sitting on a table, dresser, counter, etc. and I am standing. Some while receiving oral sex. Some from behind while I manually stimulate them as well.

—*Government employee administration, 32*

...there is no desire to bring her to orgasm either quickly or strongly, but when that moment simply is held suspended, and in gradual increments, released, and released, and released...get the point?
—*Therapist, 50*

Ummm....that's a hard one...
—*Building restoration worker, 37*

After a fun bit of foreplay (and, no, not just getting naked, f-o-r-e-p-l-a-y), cunnilingus usually works fastest. It depends, though. Some women don't like oral sex at all.
—*Healthcare provider, 26*

She just plain lets go. If a woman is really hot and worked up and in the mood and goes for it, it can be a wild ride. I've actually listened to a woman have an orgasm on the phone (a friend of mine who wanted to share) and she wanted so much to feel so good right then, she just had a blast. Gee, come to think of it, I wish that would happen more often.
—*Advertising project manager, 26*

MY THOUGHTS ON BRINGING A *Woman* TO ORGASM ARE...

MY

THOUGHTS

ON

BRINGING

A *Woman*

TO ORGASM

ARE...

Every woman has a different position, spot, etc. The last few women never got to orgasm. After several attempts and coaching, it still never happened. Their loss, I guess.
—*Architect, 33*

I've talked to her, told her how desirable she is, how much I love her body...graphically... and touched and kissed and tasted every part of her. I've had a woman have an orgasm simply from sucking her nipples, but this has been after we've made love many times.
—*Designer, 47*

She really wants to be there.
—*Pharmacist, 48*

She lets you know what really turns her on...honestly...and she must trust the man... and let go...
—*Art director, 43*

She's had a nice, long massage…

—Media consultant, 42

She has a strong attraction to me… plus the angle of penetration.

—Optician, 48

She is in total, 100 percent, unconditional love.

—Compliance analyst, 24

You spend a lot of time in verbal or nonsexual fore-play.

—Corporate manager, 41

Every woman is different, but generally my oral sex brings on the quickest "O."

—Information systems analyst, 30

She does it herself.

—Firefighter, 43

MY

THOUGHTS

ON

BRINGING

A *Woman*

TO ORGASM

ARE…

The guy does two simple things that require discipline. First, he has to take his time and find his partner's natural rhythm. Second, he has to approach sex with the perspective of pleasing his partner first. Do these couple of things and bet the house he's going to be a happy guy within minutes.

—*Accountant, 34*

MY

THOUGHTS

ON

BRINGING

A *Woman*

TO ORGASM

ARE...